ESSENTIAL
WORSHIP GUITAR

INSTRUCTION FOR
THE WORSHIP MUSICIAN

SANDY HOFFMAN

Emerald
Books

P.O. Box 635
Lynnwood, WA 98046

Emerald Books are distributed through YWAM Publishing. For a full list of titles, including other worship resources, visit our website at www.ywampublishing.com.

Essential Worship Guitar:
Instruction for the Worship Musician

Published by Emerald Books
P.O. Box 635
Lynnwood, Washington 98046

ISBN 1-883002-73-7

10 09 08 07 06 05   10 9 8 7 6 5 4 3 2

Scripture quotations in this book are taken from the New King James Version, Copyright © 1979, 1980, 1982 by Thomas Nelson, Inc., Publishers. Used by permission.

Printed in the United States of America.

DEDICATION

To my wonderful parents, Sam and Barbara Hoffman.

es•sen•tial (e sen´chul):

of or constituting the intrinsic, fundamental
nature of something; basic; absolutely necessary;
indispensable; requisite

CONTENTS

*indicates proficiency exercises

SECTION III. ATTACKS

SECTION IV. PROGRESSIONS

SECTION V. KEYS

SECTION VI. SINGLE NOTES

SECTION VII. IMPROVISING

APPENDICES

INDEX I. SONGS AND MUSICAL TERMS

INDEX II. CHORD DIAGRAMS

IN CLOSING

FOREWORD by Karen Lafferty

From the time that mankind first began to form the "essential" elements of culture and society, there was music. Adam learned farming to feed his family. Jabal tended livestock and used animal hides to make tents. Tubal-Cain discovered how to forge many useful implements of bronze and iron. But even with the development of all these practical skills, something was missing. We are told in Genesis four that "Jubal was the father of those who play the flute and lyre." Why was music so essential to the growth of culture and society? The answer lies in the fundamental truth that God created man and woman in His image...to be creative...to love beauty...to express emotion. And God also put in the spirit of humankind the desire to worship. Music facilitates all of the above; and having the means at our disposal to express that worship to the one True God, our creator, is essential for us if we are to live life to its fullest.

My association with Sandy Hoffman has helped me to understand these truths in a deeper way. He has an enthusiasm to worship God in truth and with skill, emotion, and beauty. He not only endeavors to do this himself but desires to help others discover the joy of passionate worship!

Although all of the books in the *Essential Worship* series ARE essential, I must rate the *Essential Worship Guitar* book as number ONE. This is not just because I am a guitarist myself and have learned much from this book, it's because the guitar is such a versatile and practical instrument. It is one of the easiest instruments to transport and does not have to have electricity to be heard. It can also function as "the whole band;" producing solid bass lines, exciting rhythms, beautiful harmonies, "cool" solos, and extreme dynamics! And it can do this in a wide variety of styles when the player has learned to find his or her way around the instrument. Sandy has labored to make the *Essential Worship Guitar* book a practical and fun tool that will help any diligent guitarist "find their way."

The Lord has admonished us many times in Scripture to "praise the Lord on the stringed instrument." As you discover and learn from this book, I pray that you not only have a good time improving your skills but that you will also ask the Holy Spirit to impart to you the passion for worshiping God that I have seen in the one who compiled this book. Sandy Hoffman is a man who sincerely and skillfully worships God.

A fellow worshiper,

Karen Lafferty

Recording artist/composer and founder of Musicians For Missions International, a ministry of Youth With A Mission, Santa Fe, NM

INTRODUCTION

Like anything worth waiting for, the *Essential Worship Guitar* book has been many years in the making. From my earliest experiences as a worship leader I have desired to share this knowledge with others who, like myself, have longed to worship God with their instruments.

Essential Worship Guitar is a compilation of knowledge acquired during the past 17 years of worship leading and study. I pondered long over the title when I realized the pages covered so much material, thinking perhaps it might best be called "comprehensive" rather than "essential." But after careful consideration, I do not believe that any of the information presented on the following pages is non-essential to the worship guitarist.

The book is laid out in seven sections which move in a logical progression from basic chord construction to improvisation by inspiration. Along the way the guitarist is exposed to chart anatomy, strumming and finger picking skills, "free worship" chord progressions, key changes, and basic scales and modes. Also included are appendix items such as guitar finger board notes and "Ten Top Tips for Tight Teams."

I trust that as you move prayerfully through the technical information in this book, the Holy Spirit will anoint and set you free to fully express His creative presence in the music you offer up to Him! May God multiply your spiritual/musical abilities as you invest the time to perfect these essentials of worship guitar; and may He use you mightily to worship before His throne—and to take others with you as you go!

Sing to Him a new song; **play skillfully** *with a shout of joy.*
Psalm 33:3

Sandy Hoffman

I. CHORDS

ABOUT CHORD CONSTRUCTION

I.   **The chords in any key are constructed with notes diatonic (or relating) to that key.***

The notes in the C major scale are: C, D, E, F, G, A, B. The major chords in the key of C are constructed with combinations of these notes.

II.   **A chord is three or more notes played at the same time. (Two notes played together are considered to be a "double stop.")**

To build the C major chord, simply play the 1st, 3rd, and 5th notes of the C major scale at the same time (C, E, G).

III.   **Notes in a chord may be repeated within that chord.**

On the guitar the most common form of the C major chord is spelled C, E, G, C, E. This means that the notes C and E are repeated in the chord voicing. The two C's are one "octave," or eight notes apart, as are the two E's.

Think:

do	re	mi	fa	so	la	ti	do	re	mi
C	D	**E**	F	G	A	B	**C**	D	**E**
1	2	**3**	4	5	6	7	**8** (1)		
		1	2	3	4	5	6	7	**8** (1)

IV.   **Notes moved one half-step to the next highest position or "fret" are considered to be "sharp" (#).**

V.   **Notes moved one half-step to the next lowest position or "fret" are considered to be "flat" (♭).**

---

*For a broader understanding of common chord construction in <u>every key</u> it is recommended that the student purchase a guitar chord book or dictionary.

COMMON CHORD CONSTRUCTION
(Built on a "C" root or bass note)

C Major Scale Note Number:	1	2	3	4	5	6	7	1 (8)
C Major Scale Note Name:	C	D	E	F	G	A	B	C
Half-Steps Between Notes:		2	2	1	2	2	2	1

	Chord Type:	Note Intervals:					Chord Name:
1.	MAJOR:	1	3	5			C
2.	MINOR	1	♭3	5			Cm
3.	DIMINISHED	1	♭3	♭5			CDim
4.	AUGMENTED:	1	3	#5			CAug
5.	MAJOR 7th:	1	3	5	7		CMaj7
6.	MINOR 7th:	1	♭3	5	♭7		Cm7
7.	DOMINANT 7th:	1	3	5	♭7		C7
8.	MAJOR 9th:	1	3	5	7	9	CMaj9
9.	MINOR 9th:	1	♭3	5	♭7	9	Cm9
10.	DOMINANT 9th:	1	3	5	♭7	9	C9
11.	1/2 (one over two)	1	3	5	/2 (bass note)		C/D
	(see Alternate Bass Notes, pp. 7 & 8)						
12.	6th:	1	3	6			C6
13.	2:	1	2	5			C2
	(see 2 Chords and add9 Chords, pp. 4 & 5)						
14.	add9:	1	3	5	9		Cadd9
	(see 2 Chords and add9 Chords, pp. 4 & 5)						
15.	4:	1	4	5			C4
	(SUS)	*(see 4 Chords, p. 6)*					

COMMON CHORD CONSTRUCTION

refer to COMMON CHORD CONSTRUCTION *(page 2)*

1. **C**

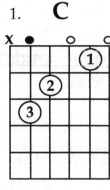

2. **Cm**

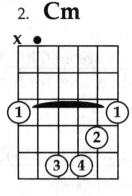

3. **CDim**

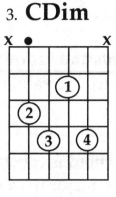

4. **CAug**

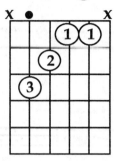

5. **CMaj7**

6. **Cm7**

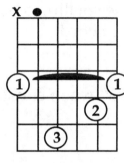

7. **C7**

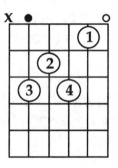

8. **CMaj9**

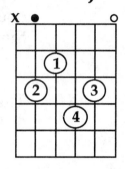

9. **Cm9**

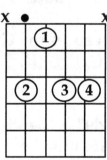

10. **C9**

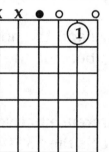

11. **C/D** (1/2)

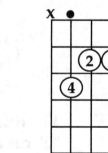

12. **C6**

13. **C2**

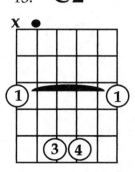

14. **Cadd9**

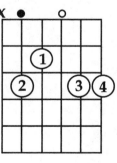

15. **C4**

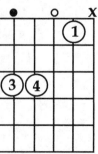

x = do not play   o = play open   • = root (bass) note   = barre chord

ABOUT "2" CHORDS & "Add9" CHORDS

I.　　"2" chords and "add9" chords are also known as "color chords" and as such are valuable substitutes for the major triad.

II.　　The "2" chord is constructed by lowering the note which is the 3rd in the major triad one whole step.

　　　The C major triad is spelled C, E, G. By lowering the 3rd (E) one whole step we change the spelling to C, D, G. This causes the C chord to become the C2 chord.

III.　　The "2" always cancels the "3" when constructing a "2" chord. (1, 3, 5 - 3 + 2 = "2" chord)

IV.　　The "add9" chord is constructed by adding the note occupying the ninth scale degree to the major triad. (1, 3, 5 + 9 = "add9")

　　　When we add the note D to the C major triad this causes the C chord to become the Cadd9. This chord is spelled C, E, G, D.

V.　　The difference between the "2" chord and the "add9" is that the "2" cancels the "3" (C, D, G) while the "add9" maintains the "3" (C, E, G, D).

"2" CHORDS and "Add9" CHORDS

Cadd9

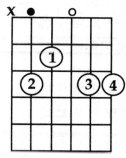

C2

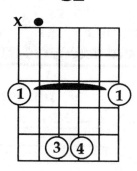

Dadd9

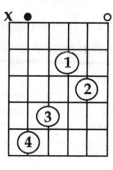

D 2

Eadd9

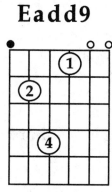

E2

7 fr.

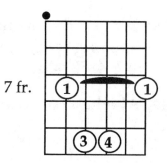

Fadd9

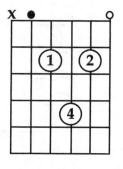

F2

Gadd9

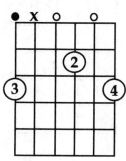

G2

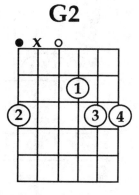

Aadd9

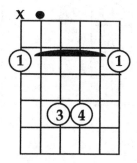

A2

Badd9

7 fr.

B2

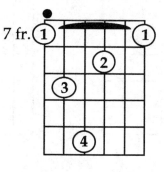

x = do not play   o = play open   ● = root (bass) note   7 fr. = fret number

ABOUT "4" CHORDS

I.   Like the "2" and "add9" chords, the "4" chord is a color chord.

II. Although it can be substitutionary, the "4" chord is a suspension chord and if not resolved, the listener is left hanging.

Occasionally a composer will end a phrase or composition with a "4" chord. This device is used when musical tension is desired.

III. The "4" chord is constructed by raising the note which is the 3rd in the major triad one half step.

The C major triad is spelled C, E, G. By raising the 3rd (E) one half-step we change the spelling to C, F, G. This causes the C chord to become the C4 chord.

IV. The "4" always cancels the "3" when constructing a "4" chord. (1, 3, 5 - 3 + 4 = "4" chord)

C4

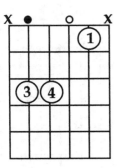

D4

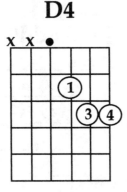

E4

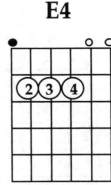

F4

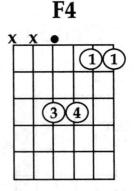

G4

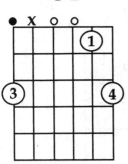

A4

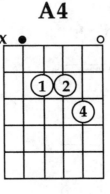

B 4

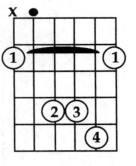

x = do not play   o = play open   • = root (bass) note   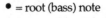 = barre chord

ABOUT ALTERNATE BASS NOTES

I.   **Alternate bass notes are yet another way to add "color" to chords. They can add a sense of linear movement or activity to an otherwise "stationary" musical moment.**

II.   **The most often used alternate to the bass or "root" note of a major chord is the 5th of the chord, dropped or inverted an octave.** (see ABOUT INVERSIONS, p. 20)

    The C chord is spelled C, E, G. If we lower the G an octave, we have placed it in the lowest pitch position of the chord. This means we're using it as an alternate bass note (G, C, E). This chord is communicated as C/G or "C over G".

III.   **The alternate bass can also be used as a "tension and release" device. This is especially effective when moving from the 3rd of the major chord (dropped an octave) back to the root of the chord.**

    Try playing the C/E chord: (that's…E, C, E, G, C, E) on the guitar in first position, then resolve it to the standard C chord: C, E, G, C, E.

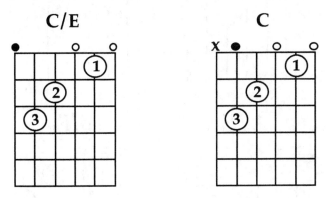

IV.   **When playing with other musicians, it's best to have only the bass guitar play the moving or alternate bass parts. This helps to avoid conflicting low frequencies (mud) and gives each instrument its own aural identity in the mix.**

ALTERNATE BASS NOTES (using 3rds & 5ths)

C/E
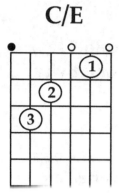

D/F#
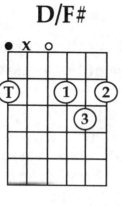

E/G#
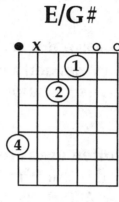

F/A
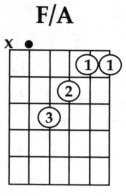

G/B
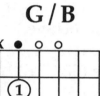

A/C#
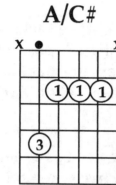

B/D#
4 fr.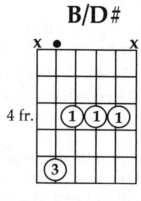

C/G
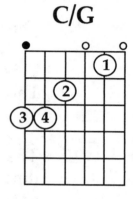

D/A
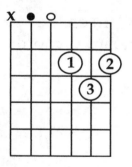

E/B
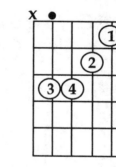

F/C

G/D
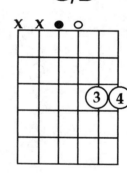

A/E
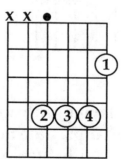

B/F#

ALTERNATE BASS CHALLENGE

♩ = 80

finger picking style:

Songs of Deliverance

Samuel Hoffman

Songs of Deliverance—chord diagrams

G
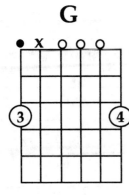

G4
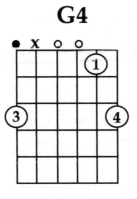

Cadd9
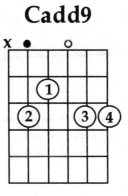

G/B
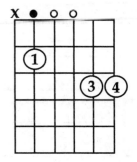

D4
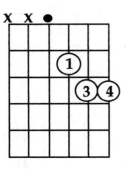

Am7
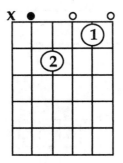

C/D
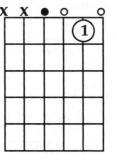

G2/B
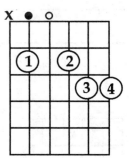

x = do not play   o = play open   ● = root (bass) note

YOUR NOTES:

♪♪ ♩ ♩ ♪♪

ABOUT OPEN CHORD VOICINGS

I.   **Open chord voicings tend to make the fullest use of the sonic capabilities of the guitar. By allowing as many simultaneously open strings to ring as possible, the listener is able to enjoy the sound of the instrument at its resonant best.**

II.   **Open voicings in the key of E allow for a constant "droning" of the open B and E strings. This provides many opportunities for tension/release and dissonant/harmonic contrasts.**

When playing an E to A2 to B4 to E chord progression, there is a noticeable change from harmonic to dissonant and back to harmonic. Changing chords from B4 to E demonstrates the move from tension to release; from suspension to a type of resolution.

III.   **Open voicings in the key of E also allow for ease in playing some full chordal scales. Try the following:**

E, A2/F#, E2/G#, A2, E/B, A2/C#, B4/D#, Aadd9/E
(see "OPEN E" CHORDED SCALE, pp. 14 & 15)

"OPEN E" CHORD VOICINGS

E
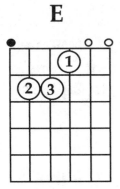

A2/F#
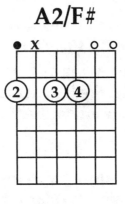

E2/G#
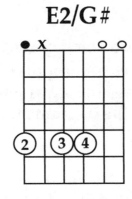

A2
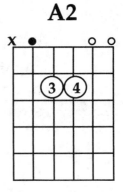

E / B
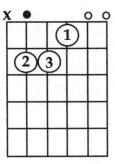

A2/C#
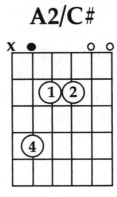

B4/D#
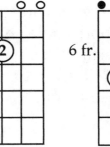

Aadd9/E
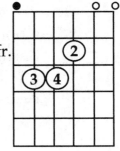

D6add9
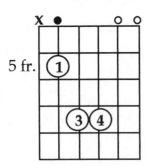

D 2
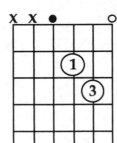

Eno3
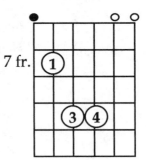

x = do not play   o = play open   ● = root (bass) note   4 fr. = fret number

"OPEN E" CHORDED SCALE

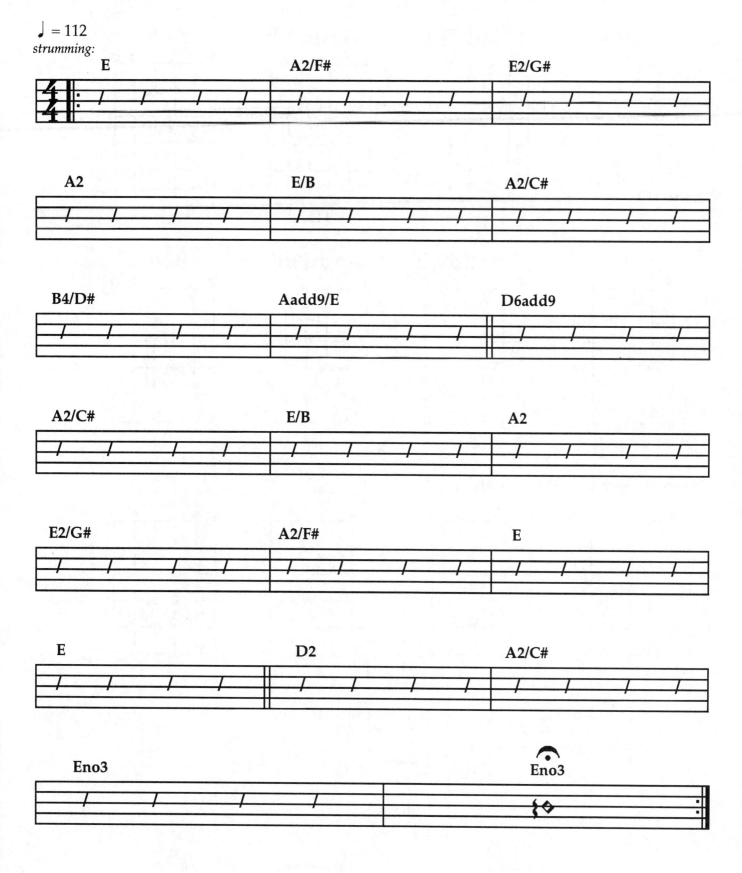

MORE OPEN CHORD VOICINGS - (Key of "E")

Eno3
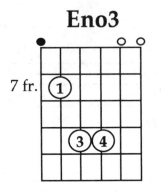
7 fr.

D6add9/E
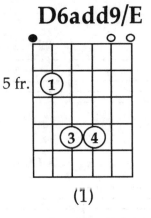
5 fr.

(1)

Aadd9/E
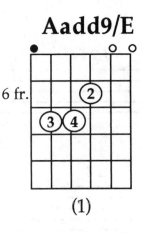
6 fr.

(1)

B4/E
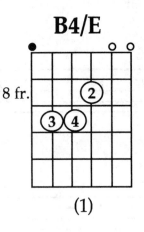
8 fr.

(1)

E
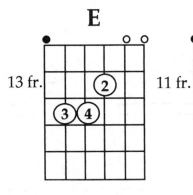
13 fr.

D6add9/E
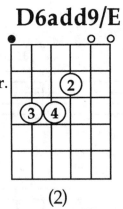
11 fr.

(2)

Aadd9/E
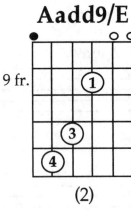
9 fr.

(2)

B4/E
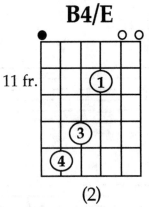
11 fr.

(2)

A2/F#
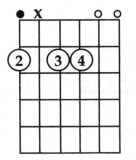

E2/G#
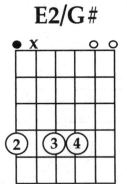

A2
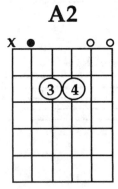

B4
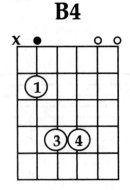

E2
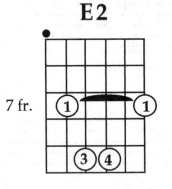
7 fr.

x = do not play   o = play open   ● = root (bass) note   7 fr. = fret number

OPEN CHORD CHALLENGE

♩ = 140

strumming:

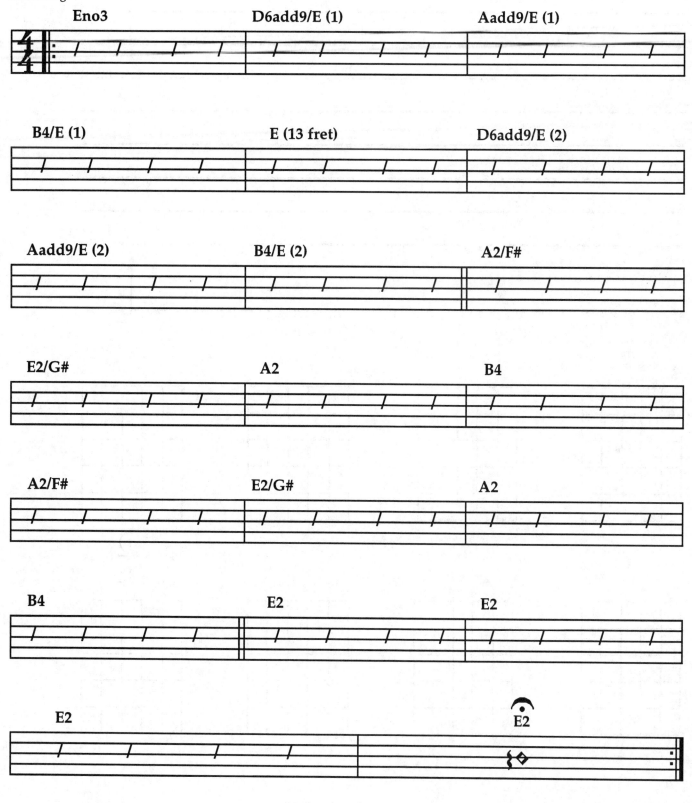

YOUR NOTES: ♫♪ ♩ ♩ ♫♪

ABOUT INTERVALS

I.   **The notes in a chord are separated from one another by spaces called intervals.**

II.   **Intervals are measured in numbers of "half-steps."**

Two half-steps are equal to one whole step. From C to C# is one half-step and from C# to D is one half-step. Therefore, from C to D is one whole step.

III. **On the guitar, one half-step is the distance from one fret to the next. It is also one half-step from the fourth fret of one string to the next highest open string. (The only exception being the G or third string which moves one half-step from its third fret, B flat, to the next highest open string, B.)**

The notes in the first 7 frets of the low E string of the guitar progress as follows:

Open	1st	2nd	3rd	4th	5th	6th	7th
E	**F**	**F#**	**G**	**G#**	**A**	**A#**	**B**
half-step	half-step	half-step	half-step	half-step	half-step	half-step	

ABOUT INVERSIONS

I.   **To construct an inverted chord, we build the chord on a diatonic note *other than* the root note of the chord.**

The G major chord is spelled G, B, D (**root** position).

To construct a **first inversion** of the G major chord we begin with the note B (two whole steps above the root) and spell the chord B, D, G. The lowest note has now become the highest.

To construct a **second inversion** of the G major chord we begin with the note D (three and one-half steps above the root) and spell the chord D, G, B. Once again the lowest note has become the highest.

Root position G major: G, B, D   (G chord)

First inversion G major: B, D, G   (G/B chord)

Second inversion G major: D, G, B   (G/D chord)

CHORDS IN THREE POSITIONS

FOURTH STRING ROOT:

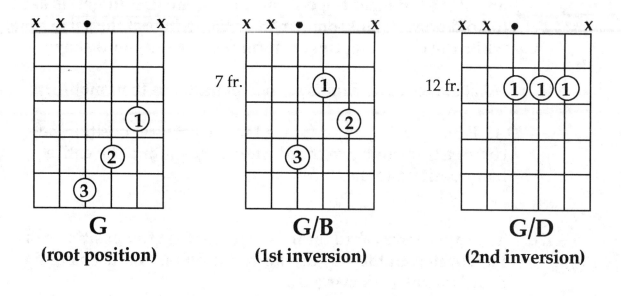

G
(root position)

G/B
(1st inversion)

G/D
(2nd inversion)

THIRD STRING ROOT:

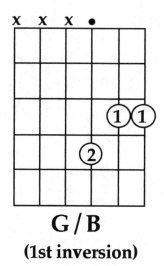

G / B
(1st inversion)

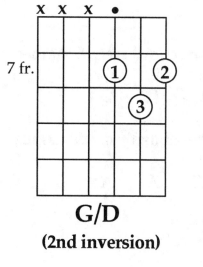

G/D
(2nd inversion)

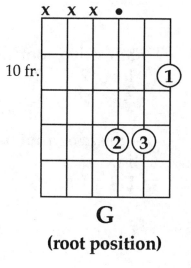

G
(root position)

x = do not play   o = play open   • = root (bass) note   7 fr. = fret number

ABOUT BARRE CHORDS

I. The most obvious shared characteristic of barre chords is that one of the left hand fingers (most often the first finger) is used to hold down (stop) some or all of the strings at the same time, while the remaining fingers form the desired chord shape.

II. What makes barre chords so indispensable is their mobility.

An F major barre chord (played in the first fret position)becomes a G major barre chord simply by shifting the entire hand position to the third fret.

III. The same barre chord form used in the first fret position can be repeated all the way up the guitar finger board, changing chord names with every fret.

IV. The two most common bass or root note locations of the barre chord are the 5th string root and the 6th string root.

5th string root barre chord frets & names:

1	2	3	4	5	6	7	8	9	10	11	12
A#	B	C	C#	D	D#	E	F	F#	G	G#	A

6th string root barre chord frets & names:

1	2	3	4	5	6	7	8	9	10	11	12
F	F#	G	G#	A	A#	B	C	C#	D	D#	E

BARRE CHORDS: 5TH STRING ROOT

C

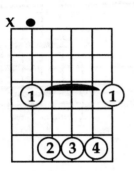

C2

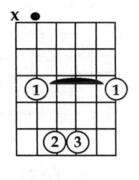

C4

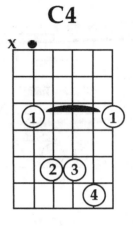

C7

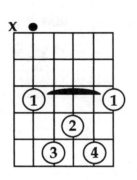

C Maj7

C/D

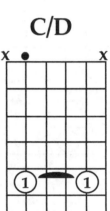

C m

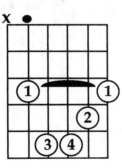

Cm7

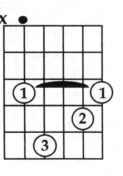

x = do not play   ● = root (bass) note   ⬛ = barre chord

BARRE CHORDS: 6TH STRING ROOT

G
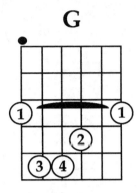

Gadd9
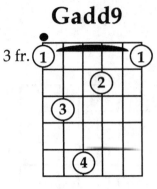

G4
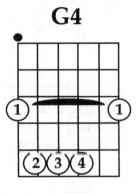

G7
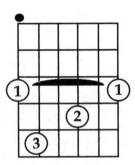

G Maj7
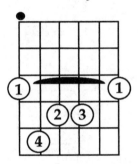

G/A
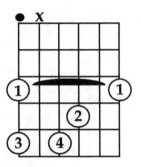

G m
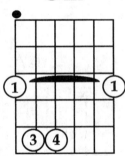

Gm7
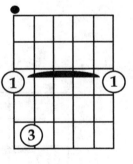

x = do not play　　　　　3 fr. = fret number　　　　　● = root (bass) note　　　　 = barre chord

II. ANATOMY

ABOUT CHARTS

I.   **The language of music is communicated in many different forms. There are lead sheets, charts, full music scores (usually piano parts or full orchestration) and the chord/lyric sheet with chord names written above the words.** *(see pp. 29–32)*

Though the chord/lyric sheet seems to be one of the most popular forms of worship music communication, it is very lacking in detail. Therefore:

II.   **This section on chart anatomy is included to broaden the scope of your understanding and consequently improve your ability to communicate musically.**

III.   **The definition of "chart" is broad and encompasses many communication forms. For our purposes a chart will consist of** *a series of musical symbols (anatomy) which give detailed information about a piece of music.* **While the chart may** *not* **include lyrics, with a little experience anyone who can count to four can read a chart.**

IV.   **For the sake of comparison and clarity, we will take a look at lead sheets (these include the lyrics, melody line, and chord names) charts (these include chord names and rhythmic notation) and chord/lyric sheets (these include the lyrics and chord names).**

ANATOMY OF A CHART

1.	♩ = 136	tempo marking (indicates beats per minute)
2.	𝄞	treble clef sign
3.	𝄢	bass clef sign
4.	♯ **or** ♭	key signature (indicates sharps or flats in the key)
5.	$\frac{4}{4}$	time signature (indicates number of beats per measure & type of note receiving one beat)
6.	[A]	section marker (for verse, chorus, bridge, tag, etc.)
7.	**INTRO**	section heading
8.	TAG	a repeated ending (usually four bars)
9.	**Mod.**	modulate (move to a higher key)
10.	N. C.	no chord (single notes only)
11.	GTR.	indicates which instrument plays a particular passage (usually notated)
12.	8VA	play passage an octave higher or lower as indicated
13.	**Rit.**	ritard (slow tempo gradually)
14.	𝄐	"Bird's Eye" (hold the note extra long as in a pause)

15.	♩ ♩ ♩ ♩	staccato (play note or chord short and detached)
16.	♩	accent (indicates strong attack on note or chord)
17.	*f*	loud dynamic marking (forte)
18.	*p*	soft dynamic marking (piano)
19.	◁	crescendo (gradually getting louder)
20.	▷	decrescendo (gradually getting softer)
21.	**Vamp**	play the passage over and over until cue to proceed (usually by the worship leader)
22.	‖	double bar (separates sections)
23.	‖	double bar (marks the end of a section)
24.	‖: :‖	repeat sign(s) (repeat the music between the dots)
25.	1. :‖	first ending
	2. ‖	second ending
26.	/ / / /	play straight rhythm (four beats)

27.	♩♫♩♩	play the rhythm as indicated
28.	/ / ✓ /	"punch" the chord 1/2 beat early (this constitutes a syncopated rhythm)
29.	◇ or ◇	"diamond" (hold the note for its full value)
30.	./.	repeat phrase over the same number of bars
31.	𝄋	**D.S.** symbol
32.	⊕	**Coda** symbol (special ending or concluding section)
33.	**D.S. al Coda**	return to the **D.S.** symbol, then play until **"To Coda,"** then proceed to play the **Coda** (marked by **Coda** symbol)
34.	**D.S. al Fine**	return to the **D.S.** symbol and play until you reach **Fine** (pronounced: fee–nay)
35.	**D.C. al Fine**	return to the beginning of the piece and play until you reach **Fine**
36.	**Fine**	the end
37.	**S**	"slide" from one note to the next
38.	**H**	"hammer on" (strike the note with the left hand finger)
39.	**P**	"pull off" (from an already ringing note, pluck the open string with the left hand finger)
40.	⌇	"broken chord" (play chord one string at a time)

LEAD SHEET—Take Me There

Samuel Hoffman

Take Me There—chord diagrams

Gno3
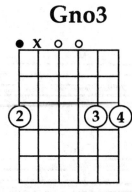

A7
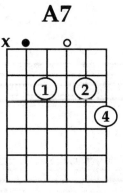

Cadd9
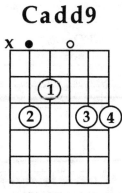

D4
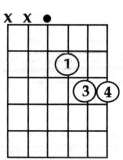

Gno3/F#
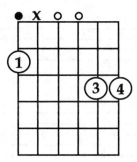

Em7
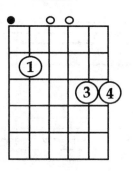

D
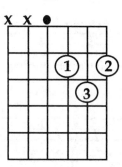

x = do not play   o = play open   ● = root (bass) note

CHART—Take Me There

♩ = 140

Hoffman

CHORD/LYRIC SHEET

TAKE ME THERE

Samuel Hoffman

INTRO: **Gno3**   **A7**   **Cadd9**   **Gno3**
           / / / /   / / / /   / / / /   / / / /

CHORUS:
           Gno3   **A7**
Take me there, let me rest
        Cadd9   **Gno3**
In that secret place with You
          Gno3   **A7**
By Your side, so satisfied
        Cadd9 D4   **Gno3**   **(Gno3/F#)**
In that secret place with You   /

VERSE 1:
Em7   **D4**   **D**
Hide me in Your holy presence
Cadd9   **Gno3**   **Gno3/F#**
Sanctuary of the heart   /
Em7   **D4**   **D**
My desire is just to be with You
     Cadd9
Forever, Lord
    D4
Forever, Lord

VERSE 2:
Em7   **D4**   **D**
Lead me to Your light, embrace me
Cadd9   **Gno3**   **Gno3/F#**
In Your everlasting love   /
Em7   **D4**   **D**
Keep me close so I can hear Your heart
     Cadd9
Forever, Lord
    D4
Forever, Lord

YOUR NOTES:

♪♪ ♩ ♩ ♪♪

III. ATTACKS

ABOUT STRUMMING

I.   **Strumming the guitar is accomplished with a pick (plectrum) or the bare fingers.**

II.   **The pick is held between the right hand thumb and index finger and is manipulated in various rhythmic combinations using down (⊓) and up (∨) strokes.**

III.   **Rhythmic notation is communicated through simple quarter note strokes: / / / /, or by more complex rhythm notation.**
                               1 2 3 4

IV.   **The values of common notes and rests used in rhythm notation in 4/4 time are as follows:**

	Note:	Rest:	Value:
whole	◇	▬	4 beats
half	◊	▬	2 beats
quarter	♩	ξ	1 beat
dotted quarter	♩.	ξ.	1 1/2 beats
eighth(s)	♫	♽	1/2 beat (each)

V.   **A "choke strum" involves striking the strings with the outside of the right hand *and* the pick at the same time. This is done in such a manner that it deadens all the strings and causes them to make a percussive sound.**

COMMON GUITAR RHYTHM PATTERNS

pick your own chords and tempos

Sing the Song of Heaven

Samuel Hoffman/Diane Wigstone

Sing the Song of Heaven—chord diagrams

Gno3
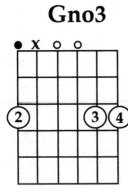

F/G
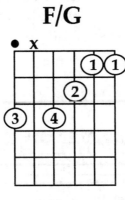

F2/ G
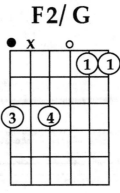

Am7
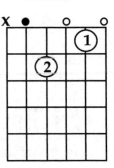

D
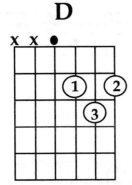

F
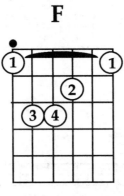

C
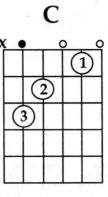

D4
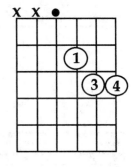

G/B
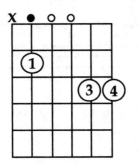

Cadd9
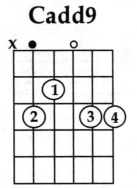

C/D

x = do not play   o = play open   • = root (bass) note   = barre chord

Sing the Song of Heaven (CHALLENGE)
(guitar rhythm chart: 1-verse, 2-bridge, 3-chorus)

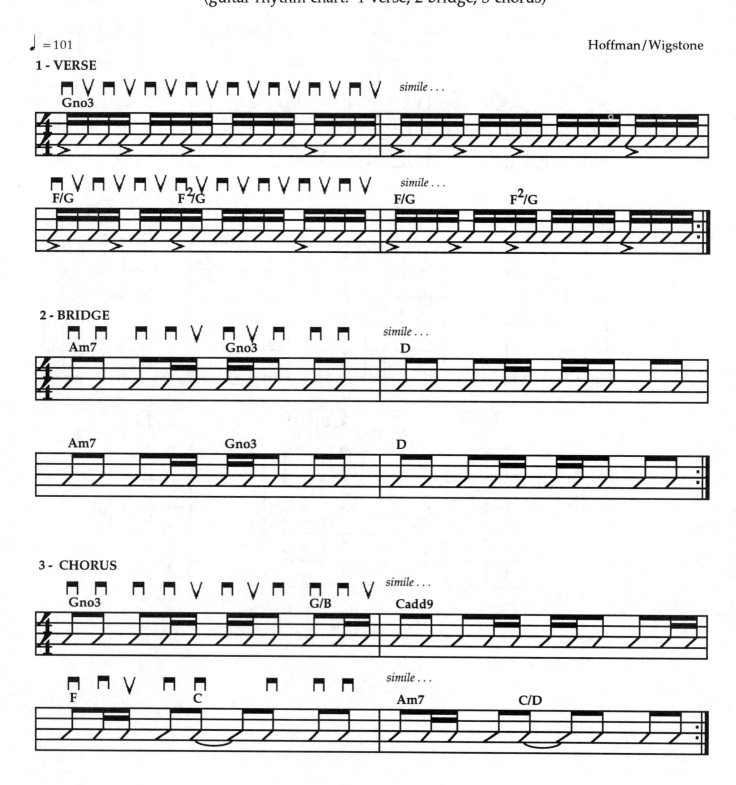

Strum/Bass/Choke Challenge

(guitar rhythm chart: choke on 2 and 4 throughout)

(*N.C. = NO CHORD - notes only)

ABOUT FINGER PICKING GUITAR

I.   Finger picking the guitar allows for great flexibility of expression on the instrument. With experience, one is actually able to play the bass, rhythm, and melody lines simultaneously.

II.   For our purposes, we will cover accompaniment styles of finger picking. These are used to back up the vocal part of a song. The patterns are usually in the form of arpeggios or "broken chords."

III.   For finger picking notation, the fingers of the right hand are designated as thumb, one, two, and three. *(T, 1, 2, 3)*

IV.   The corresponding string number, one to six, will appear beneath the right hand finger number in the "Common Finger Picking Patterns" (see example). *Remember: the smallest string is number one.*

Example:

T	1	2	3		T	1	2	3	**right hand**
6	3	2	1		6	3	2	1	**string number**
1	**2**	**3**	**4**		**1**	**2**	**3**	**4**	**beat number**

V.   It is often advantageous to switch back and forth between flat picking and finger picking. To accomplish this technique, it is necessary to learn to "finger pick" using the pick held between the right hand thumb and first finger, and alternating with the second finger of the right hand. A "P" will be used to designate when we use the pick to "finger pick." (A variation of this is to hold the pick between the first and second right hand fingers, and then "finger pick" by alternating between the thumb and second finger.) The guitarist should become proficient at both!

Example:

T/P	T/P	2	T/P		T/P	T/P	2	T/P	**right hand**
6	4	1	4		6	4	1	4	**string number**
1	**2**	**3**	**4**		**1**	**2**	**3**	**4**	**beat number**

GUITAR FINGER PICKING PATTERN 1
choose your own chords and tempos

BASIC 4/4 PATTERN: (using *eighth* notes in 4/4 time)

FOR CHORDS WITH *6th STRING ROOT*: (E, F barre, G...)

T	1	T	2	T	1	T	2	(right hand finger)
6	2	4	1	5	2	4	1	(string number)
1	+	2	+	3	+	4	+	(beat number)

FOR CHORDS WITH *5th STRING ROOT*: (A, B barre, C...)

T	1	T	2	T	1	T	2	(right hand finger)
5	2	4	1	6	2	4	1	(string number)
1	+	2	+	3	+	4	+	(beat number)

FOR CHORDS WITH *4th STRING ROOT*: (D, F...)

T	1	T	2	T	1	T	2	(right hand finger)
4	2	3	1	5	2	3	1	(string number)
1	+	2	+	3	+	4	+	(beat number)

APPLIED:

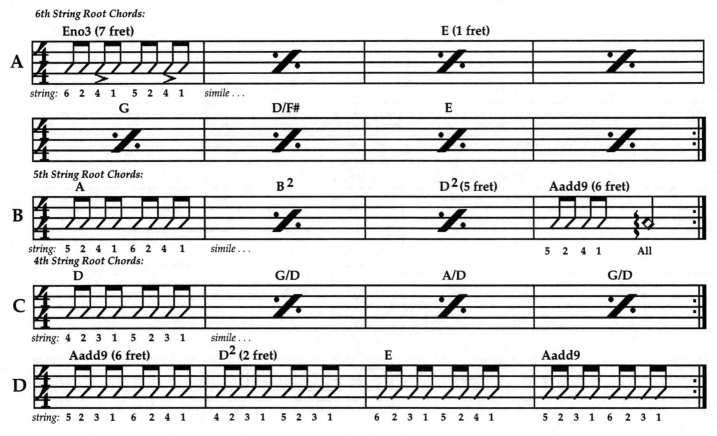

-41-

GUITAR FINGER PICKING PATTERN 2
choose your own chords and tempos

ARPEGGIOS / "WALK DOWNS": (using *quarter* notes in 4/4 time)

FOR CHORDS WITH *6th STRING ROOT:* (E, F barre, G...)

T	1	2	3	T	1	2	3	(right hand finger)
6	3	2	1	6	3	2	1	(string number)
1	2	3	4	1	2	3	4	(beat number)

FOR CHORDS WITH *5th STRING ROOT:* (A, B barre, C...)

T	1	2	3	T	1	2	3	(right hand finger)
5	3	2	1	5	3	2	1	(string number)
1	2	3	4	1	2	3	4	(beat number)

FOR CHORDS WITH *4th STRING ROOT:* (D, F...)

T	1	2	3	T	1	2	3	(right hand finger)
4	3	2	1	4	3	2	1	(string number)
1	2	3	4	1	2	3	4	(beat number)

APPLIED:

♩ = 116

C   G/B   Am   Am/G

string: 5 3 2 1   5 3 2 1   5 3 2 1   6 3 2 1

F   Dm7   F/G   G

6 3 2 1   4 3 2 1   6 3 2 1   6 3 2 1

C   G/B   Am   Am/G

5 3 2 1   5 3 2 1   5 3 2 1   6 3 2 1

F   F/G   C   C

6 3 2 1   6 3 2 1   5 3 2 1   All

GUITAR FINGER PICKING PATTERN 3

choose your own chords and tempos

BASIC 6/8 PATTERN: (using *eighth* notes in 6/8 time)

FOR CHORDS WITH *6th STRING ROOT:* (**E, F barre, G**...)

T	1	2	3	2	1	(right hand finger)
6	3	2	1	2	3	(string number)
1	2	3	4	5	6	(beat number)

FOR CHORDS WITH *5th STRING ROOT:* (**A, B barre, C**...)

T	1	2	3	2	1	(right hand finger)
5	3	2	1	2	3	(string number)
1	2	3	4	5	6	(beat number)

FOR CHORDS WITH *4th STRING ROOT:* (**D, F**...)

T	1	2	3	2	1	(right hand finger)
4	3	2	1	2	3	(string number)
1	2	3	4	5	6	(beat number)

APPLIED:

GUITAR FINGER PICKING PATTERN 4

choose your own chords and tempos

"FLAT PICK" & FINGER STYLE: (using *eighth* notes in 4/4 time)

FOR CHORDS WITH *6th STRING ROOT:* (E, F barre, G...)

T/P	T/P	2	T/P	T/P	T/P	2	T/P	(right hand finger or pick)
6	4	1/2/3 *	4	6	4	1/2/3 *	4	(string number)
1	+	2	+	3	+	4	+	(beat number)

* "brush up" with 2nd finger

FOR CHORDS WITH *5th STRING ROOT:* (A, B barre, C...)

T/P	T/P	2	T/P	T/P	T/P	2	T/P	(right hand finger or pick)
5	4	1/2/3	4	5	4	1/2/3	4	(string number)
1	+	2	+	3	+	4	+	(beat number)

FOR CHORDS WITH *4th STRING ROOT:* (D, F...)

T/P	T/P	2	T/P	T/P	T/P	2	T/P	(right hand finger or pick)
4	3	1/2	3	4	3	1/2	3	(string number)
1	+	2	+	3	+	4	+	(beat number)

APPLIED:

♩ = 70

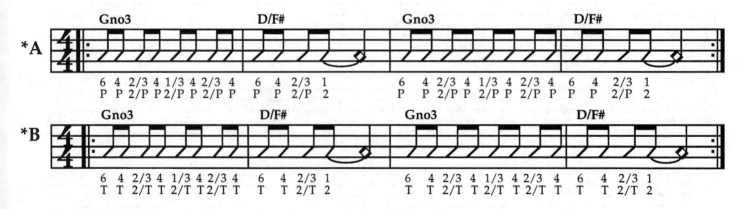

*A Using pick and second finger (p = pick)
*B Holding pick between first and second finger while using thumb and second finger (T = thumb)

Deeper In Love

Paul Baloche/Geoffrey Cuellar/
Samuel Hoffman/Ed Kerr

Deeper In Love—chord diagrams

D
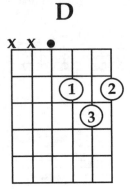

D2
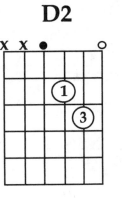

G
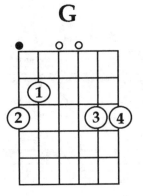

G/A
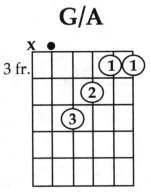

F#m7
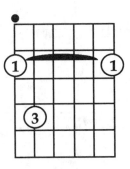

Bm
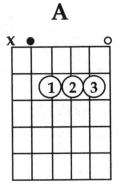

Bm/A
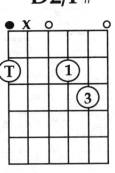

Gadd9
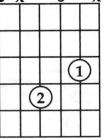

A4
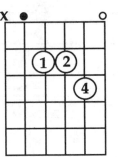

A
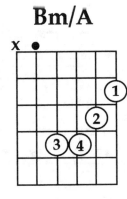

D2/F#

Em9
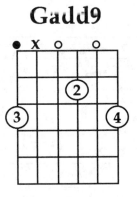

A/C#
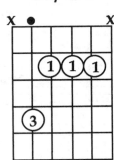

GMaj7
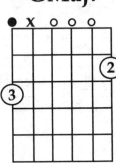

G6
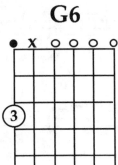

x = do not play   o = play open   • = root (bass) note   3 fr. = fret number

Deeper In Love
("free style" finger picking challenge)

♩=110   Baloche/Cuellar/Hoffman/Kerr

IV. PROGRESSIONS

ABOUT CHORD PROGRESSIONS

I.   A chord progression is a series of chords played in a predetermined sequence.

Chord:	G	C	D	G	G	C	D	G
Beat number:	**1,2**	**3,4**	**1,2**	**3,4**	**1,2**	**3,4**	**1,2**	**3,4**

II. In addition to calling chords by their letter names, G, C, D, and so on, chords can be identified by numbers. For instance, in the key of G, the G chord is chord number I. Starting with G and counting up the scale to C makes C the number IV chord and D the number V chord.

Chord:	G	A	B	C	D	E	F #	G
Chord number:	**I**	**II**	**III**	**IV**	**V**	**VI**	**VII**	**I**

III. Now instead of calling it the "G, C, D" chord progression we can identify it as the "I, IV, V" chord progression.

Chord:	G	C	D	G	G	C	D	G
Chord number:	**I**	**IV**	**V**	**I**	**I**	**IV**	**V**	**I**
Beat number:	**1,2**	**3,4**	**1,2**	**3,4**	**1,2**	**3,4**	**1,2**	**3,4**

IV. It is easy to recognize the benefit of communicating with the number system. If we use numbers instead of letters to indicate chord progressions, we are free to use the same chord progression in as many different keys as we like without ever having to rewrite the music.

Number:	I	IV	V	I		I	IV	V	I
Chord:	G	C	D	G		G	C	D	G
	C	F	G	C		C	F	G	C
	D	G	A	D		D	G	A	D
	A	D	E	A		A	D	E	A
	E	A	B	E		E	A	B	E

CHORDED SCALES IN MAJOR KEYS
a companion to COMMON CHORD PROGRESSIONS *(page 50)*

Major Key	I	IIm	IIIm	IV	V	VIm	VIIdim
C	C	Dm	Em	F	G	Am	Bdim
G	G	Am	Bm	C	D	Em	F#dim
D	D	Em	F#m	G	A	Bm	C#dim
A	A	Bm	C#m	D	E	F#m	G#dim
E	E	F#m	G#m	A	B	C#m	D#dim
B	B	C#m	D#m	E	F#	G#m	A#dim
F#	F#	G#m	A#m	B	C#	D#m	E#dim
C#	C#	D#m	E#m	F#	G#	A#m	B#dim
F	F	Gm	Am	B♭	C	Dm	Edim
B♭	B♭	Cm	Dm	E♭	F	Gm	Adim
E♭	E♭	Fm	Gm	A♭	B♭	Cm	Ddim
A♭	A♭	B♭m	Cm	D♭	E♭	Fm	Gdim
D♭	D♭	E♭m	Fm	G♭	A♭	B♭m	Cdim
G♭	G♭	A♭m	B♭m	C♭	D♭	E♭m	Fdim
C♭	C♭	D♭m	E♭m	F♭	G♭	A♭m	B♭dim

COMMON CHORD PROGRESSIONS

pick a key, then refer to the CHORDED SCALES IN MAJOR KEYS (page 49) to correlate the chords in that key with the number system chord progressions on this page

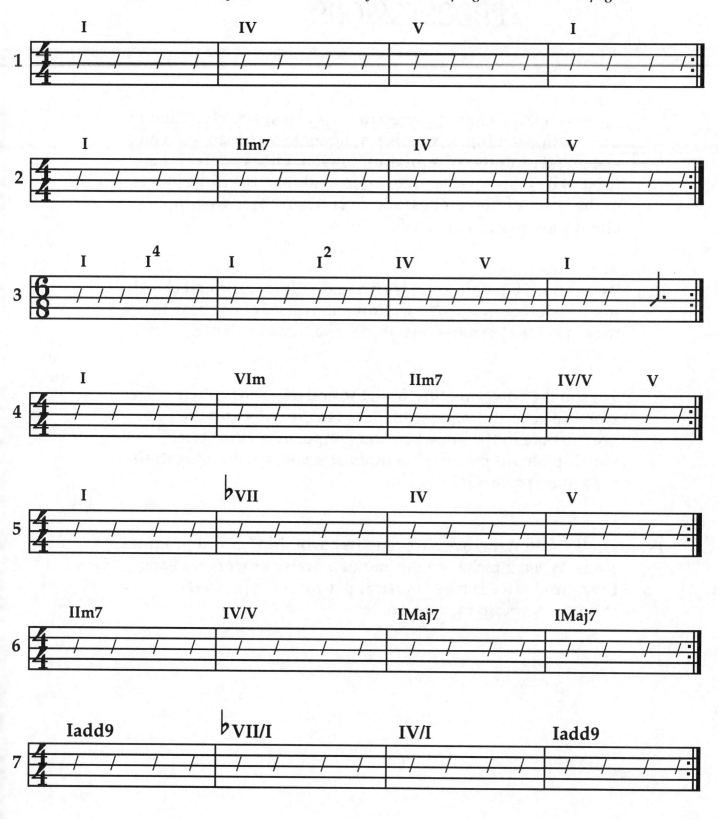

ABOUT "FREE WORSHIP" CHORD PROGRESSIONS

I.   "Free worship" chord progressions have a special function in the worship setting. A worship song makes a broad, general statement of praise or adoration to God. Often we feel the need to be more specific, more personal than the expressions of the lyrics of the composer. This is where "free worship" chord progressions are useful.

II.   By ending a worship song with a many times repeated chord progression or "vamp," we allow the worshiper(s) time to make personal expressions of praise or thanksgiving.

III.   We should flow smoothly from the end of a song into the "free worship" chord progression. Because the song and the progression are in the same key and tempo, often the "free worship" chord progression leads us back into the song itself for a more predictable finish.

IV.   On the following page are ten "free worship" chord progressions. When attached to the end of a praise or worship song they provide a seamless musical platform for personal, intimate worship expression.

FREE WORSHIP CHORD PROGRESSIONS

V. KEYS

ABOUT CHANGING KEYS
modulation

I.   Changing keys (modulating) especially in the praise and worship arena, is a valuable device for building interesting song arrangements. Key changes can *also* be used to move seamlessly from one song to the next. (see APPENDIX I)

II.   Key changes are almost always upward, moving one half-step or one whole step from the old key to the new key.

III.   Modulation is often accomplished with the use of a pivotal chord (4/5) having characteristics common to the old key and the new.

In the key of C, the G chord is the number V chord. In the key of D, the G chord is the number IV chord. To move from the key of C to the key of D, we use the G chord (which is common to both keys) and place it over the number V *note* (A) in the new key. This "4/5" chord (G/A) in the new key is both pleasing to the ear *and* functional on the theoretical level.

Old key:	I	IV	V	
	C	F	G	
Beat:	1,2	3,4	1,2	
Pivotal:	IV/V (new key)			
	G/A			
Beat:	3,4			
New key:	I	IV	V	I
	D	G	A	D
Beat:	1,2	3,4	1,2	3,4

IV.   Key changes may also be accomplished by using the dominant 7th chord of the new key in place of the 4/5. Occasionally key changes are made directly from one key to another with no pivotal chord at all.

MOVABLE 4/5 (IV/V) CHORD FORMS
pivotal chords

5th String Root: **6th String Root:**

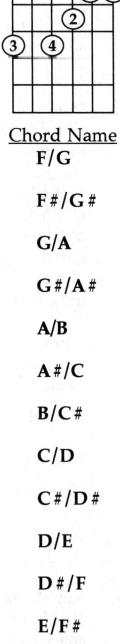

Fret Number	Chord Name	Chord Name
1.	G#/A#	F/G
2.	A/B	F#/G#
3.	A#/C	G/A
4.	B/C#	G#/A#
5.	C/D	A/B
6.	C#/D#	A#/C
7.	D/E	B/C#
8.	D#/F	C/D
9.	E/F#	C#/D#
10.	F/G	D/E
11.	F#/G#	D#/F
12.	G/A	E/F#

x = do not play   o = play open   ● = root (bass) note

CHANGING KEYS ON GUITAR
using pivotal chords (number system in parenthesis—see page 49)

♩ = 72

1

| G (I) | Cadd9 (IV) | D (V) | Cadd9 (IV) | G (I) | Cadd9 (IV) | D (V) | D/E (IV/V) |

(Pivot)

(New Key)

| A (I) | D² (IV) | E (V) | D² (IV) | A (I) | D² (IV) | E (V) | A (I) |

♪ = 155

2

| D (I) | G (IV) | A (V) | G/A (IV/V)   A/B (IV/V) |

(Pivot)

(New Key)

| E (I) | A (IV) | B (V) | E (I) |

♩ = 63

3

| G (I) | Am7 (IIm7) | C (IV) | D (V) | G (I) | Am7 (IIm7) | C (IV) | C/D-(IV/V) - D/E |

(Pivot)

(New Key)

| A (I) | Bm7 (IIm7) | D (IV) | E (V) | A (I) | Bm7 (IIm7) | D (IV)   E (V) | A (I) |

♩ = 170

4

| G (I) | C (IV) | G (I) | G (I) | C (IV) | G (I) |

(New Key)

| A (I) | D (IV)   A (I) | A (I) | D (IV)   A (I) |

♩ = 170

5

| G (I) | G (I) | E⁷ (V⁷) | E⁷ (V⁷) |

(Pivot)

(New Key)

| A (I) | D (IV) | E (V) | A (I) |

ABOUT CAPOED KEYS

I. **The use of the capo will be discussed in two forms.**

1. *You may use the capo to change the key of a song without learning the first position chords in the new key.*

If the song is in the key of E and you need to play it in the key of G, simply place the capo across the finger board, just behind the third fret bar and play the same chords you would have played in the key of E. By using the capo in the third fret, you have shortened the finger board of your instrument by three frets. This raises the pitch of the instrument one and one-half steps and causes chords played with the key of E fingerings to sound like chords in the key of G.

2. *You may use the capo to play a song in its original key but at a different location on the finger board.*

This technique is often used to give the instrument a higher sound (pitch) and thus to change the character of the piece of music. This use of the capo also works very well in situations where two guitars are playing together. While guitar 1 plays the song in first position (without capo), guitar 2 plays in a capoed position farther up the finger board. Here is a sample of the way the chords line up:

First position key of G:	G	C	D	G
Capoed Fifth fret key of G:	D (G)	G (C)	A (D)	D (G)

II. **When using a capo, always place it straight up and down and directly behind the fret (not quite on top of the fret).**

CAPOED KEY CHANGES

Using chords in the key of E, the following key changes occur as we move the capo one fret at a time from "open" position to the 7th fret:

	I	IIm	IIIm	IV	V	VIm	VIIdim
	Key of:						
"Open"	E	F#m	G#m	A	B	C#m	D#dim
	Becomes:						
Capo 1st fret	F	Gm	Am	Bb	C	Dm	Edim
	Becomes:						
Capo 2nd fret	F#	G#m	A#m	B	C#	D#m	E#dim
	Becomes:						
Capo 3rd fret	G	Am	Bm	C	D	Em	F#dim
	Becomes:						
Capo 4th fret	G#	A#m	B#m	C#	D#	E#m	Gdim
	Becomes:						
Capo 5th fret	A	Bm	C#m	D	E	F#m	G#dim
	Becomes:						
Capo 6th fret	A#	Cm	Dm	D#	F	Gm	Adim
	Becomes:						
Capo 7th fret	B	C#m	D#m	E	F#	G#m	A#dim

CAPOED SAME KEYS

The chords in each of the following keys can be played in capoed positions using the alternate chords listed for each.

Progression:	I	IV	V	I
	Key of:			
Open	G	C	D	G
	Is played:			
Capo 3rd fret	E (G)	A (C)	B (D)	E (G)
	Is played:			
Capo 5th fret	D (G)	G (C)	A (D)	D (G)
	Is played:			
Capo 7th fret	C (G)	F (C)	G (D)	C (G)

	Key of:			
Open	E	A	B	E
	Is played:			
Capo 2nd fret	D (E)	G (A)	A (B)	D (E)
	Is played:			
Capo 4th fret	C (E)	F (A)	G (B)	C (E)
	Is played:			
Capo 7th fret	A (E)	D (A)	E (B)	A (E)

	Key of:			
Open	A	D	E	A
	Is played:			
Capo 2nd fret	G (A)	C (D)	D (E)	G (A)
	Is played:			
Capo 5th fret	E (A)	A (D)	B (E)	E (A)
	Is played:			
Capo 7th fret	D (A)	G (D)	A (E)	D (A)

VI. SINGLE NOTES

ABOUT MODES

I.   Modes are a useful tool for the guitarist. They provide a starting point for building solos and improvising, and they act as a musical "compass" without which we lack direction on the path of creative musicianship.

II.   The modes are numbered one through seven, and are known by the Greek names Ionian (type 1), Dorian (type 2), Phrygian (type 3), Lydian (type 4), Mixolydian (type 5), Aeolian (type 6), and Locrian (7).

III. All seven modes can be played in any key, and each mode begins on a different "scale degree" of that key.

In the key of G, we call the Ionian the "G Ionian." As we progress through the scale degrees in the key of G, each mode has a different name and starts on a different note, but the key remains the same. The names of the modes in the key of G progress as follows:

	Name	Type	Scale degree	Starting note
G	Ionian	1	I	G
A	Dorian	2	II	A
B	Phrygian	3	III	B
C	Lydian	4	IV	C
D	Mixolydian	5	V	D
E	Aeolian	6	VI	E
F #	Locrian	7	VII	F #

IV.   Modes in any other key progress in the same relative fashion.

MODES—*diatonic to G*

G - IONIAN

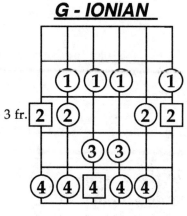

Type 1 / Scale degree I

A - DORIAN

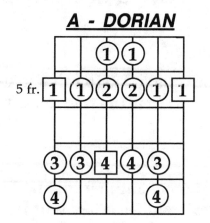

Type 2 / Scale degree II

B - PHRYGIAN

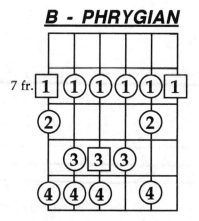

Type 3 / Scale degree III

C - LYDIAN

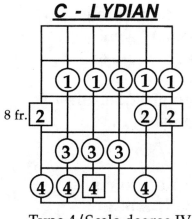

Type 4 / Scale degree IV

D - MIXOLYDIAN

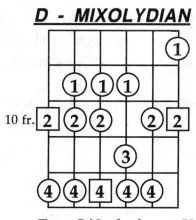

Type 5 / Scale degree V

E - AEOLIAN

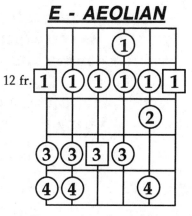

Type 6 / Scale degree VI

F# - LOCRIAN

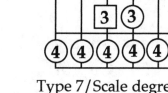

Type 7 / Scale degree VII

□ = root note of scale   3 fr. = fret number

ABOUT PENTATONIC & BLUES SCALES

I.   Pentatonic scales are played using five notes. The prefix
       "pent" added to "tonic" means five notes relating to a
       tonic (root).

II.   These types of scales are another invaluable tool in the guitar-
       ist's bag of technical goodies! They will further enable you to
       flow easily in improvisation (solos, licks, and tricks).

III.   There are both major and minor forms of the pentatonic scale.
       As you experiment with these you will recognize many well
       known musical "hooks" used over and over in popular music.

       Try playing the first six notes of the major pentatonic scale, 6th
       string root (see page 62). Do you recognize a popular "hook?"

IV.   To create a blues scale we simply add the flat five note to the
       minor pentatonic scale. This is immediately recognizable as
       the "secret ingredient" which transforms a mere minor
       pentatonic scale into something we might hear in Chicago,
       New Orleans, or on many street corners around the world.

V.   The A minor pentatonic scale is played:

       A   C   D   E   G   (A)

       1   ♭3   4   5   ♭7   (1)

       To create the A blues scale we simply add an <u>E flat</u>:

       A   C   D   <u>E flat</u>   E   G   (A)

       1   ♭3   4   ♭5   5   ♭7   (1)

PENTATONIC & BLUES SCALES
choose your own starting fret

Sixth String Root:

MAJOR PENTATONIC
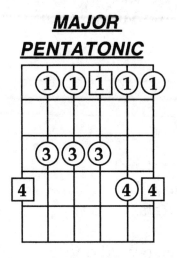

Notes: 1 - 2 - 3 - 5 - 6

(country, pop, bright)

MINOR PENTATONIC
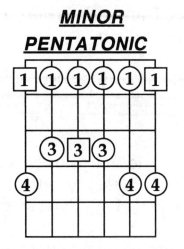

Notes: 1 - ♭3 - 4 - 5 - ♭7

(rock, pop, jazz)

BLUES FLAT 5
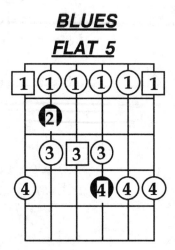

Notes: 1 - ♭3 - 4 - ♭5 - 5 - ♭7

(blues, rock, pop, jazz)

Fifth String Root:

MAJOR PENTATONIC
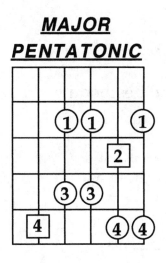

Notes: 1 - 2 - 3 - 5 - 6

(country, pop, bright)

MINOR PENTATONIC
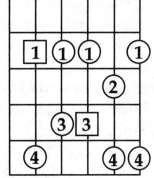

Notes: 1 - ♭3 - 4 - 5 - ♭7

(rock, pop, jazz)

BLUES FLAT 5
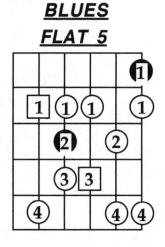

Notes: 1 - ♭3 - 4 - ♭5 - 5 - ♭7

(blues, rock, pop, jazz)

☐ = root note of scale   **②** = flat five (♭5)

ABOUT MINOR SCALES

I. **Minor scales are divided into three categories. They are the Natural Minor, Harmonic Minor, and Melodic Minor (ascending and descending).**

  The **A natural minor** scale (one octave) is:

    A B C D E F G A

  Notice that there are no sharps or flats in the A natural minor scale. This is because it is related or "relative" to "C Major" and the key of "C" has no sharps or flats.

  All major keys have a relative minor key which is located one and one-half steps down from the root note of the major key.

  (C Major to A Minor, G Major to E Minor, F Major to D Minor, etc.)

II. **To play the A harmonic minor scale (one octave) we must sharp the seven:**

    A B C D E F <u>G#</u> A

  The sharp seven occurs in both the ascending and descending Harmonic Minor scale.

III. **To play the A melodic minor scale (one octave) we must sharp the six *and* the seven (ascending) and play them as naturals when descending:**

  Ascending: **A B C D E <u>F#</u> <u>G#</u> A**

  Descending: **A <u>G</u> <u>F</u> E D C B A.**

  Notice that the descending Melodic Minor scale is the same as the Natural Minor scale.

MINOR SCALES
choose your own starting fret

Sixth String Root:

NATURAL MINOR SCALE

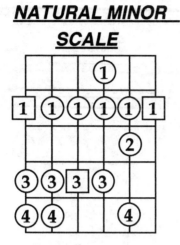

Same fingering as
AEOLIAN mode

HARMONIC MINOR SCALE

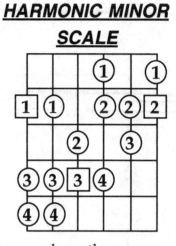

sharp the seven

MELODIC MINOR SCALE

(Ascending)

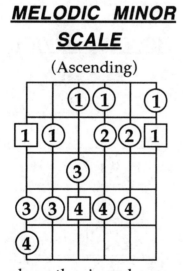

sharp the six and seven

MELODIC MINOR SCALE

(Descending)

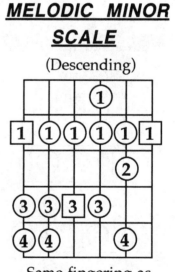

Same fingering as
NATURAL MINOR

□ = root note of scale

MINOR SCALES
choose your own starting fret

Fifth String Root:

NATURAL MINOR SCALE

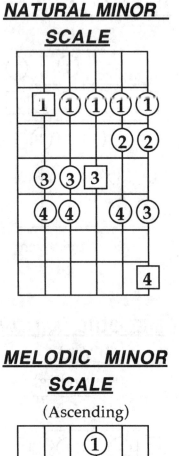

HARMONIC MINOR SCALE

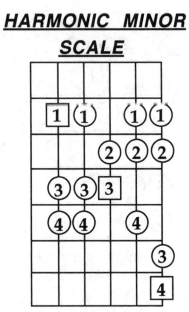

sharp the seven

MELODIC MINOR SCALE

(Ascending)

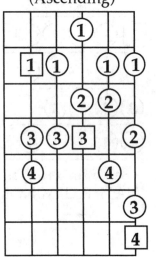

sharp the six and seven

MELODIC MINOR SCALE

(Descending)

Same notes as
NATURAL MINOR

□ = root note of scale

VII. IMPROVISING

ABOUT IMPROVISATION BY INSPIRATION

I. Improvisation by inspiration occurs when we combine technical musical knowledge with free flowing worship. This type of "spiritual musicianship" can only happen when we "recklessly abandon" our musical expression to the leadership of the Holy Spirit.

*"Moreover David and the captains of the army separated for the service some of the sons of Asaph, of Heman, and of Jeduthun, who should **prophesy** [improvisation by inspiration] with harps, stringed instruments, and cymbals. And the number of the **skilled** men performing their service was:..."*

I Chronicles 25:1

We see from this verse that they combined technical musical knowledge (they were "skilled") with the free flow of worship (they "prophesied" on their instruments).

II. The following are free worship guidelines which will help you to flow smoothly into improvisation by inspiration.

1. Be musically relevant. (quiet during quiet, etc.)
2. Remember that "less is more." Don't try to fill every musical hole. Leave space for *others* to be expressive.
3. Really know your instrument.
4. Play phrases as though you are singing. (take musical "breaths" along the way)
5. Spend plenty of time with God! Remember, it's improvisation by *inspiration!* There's only one place to get a fresh supply of that—before the throne of God.

III. On the following pages are chord progressions coupled with mode or scale suggestions. Remember, you can improvise over virtually *any* progression (even over one chord). Just stay relaxed, trust God, and allow the music to flow from the innermost depths of worship expression in your heart! Soon you'll find yourself combining all the elements of Essential Worship Guitar into one continuous expression of praise to God.

IMPROVISATIONAL CHORD PROGRESSIONS 1 & 2

choose your own keys

(Ritard last time)

IMPROVISATIONAL CHORD PROGRESSIONS 3 & 4
choose your own keys

♪ = 152   *MINOR PENTATONIC/HARMONIC MINOR*   (suggested)

3

A
| Im | IVm | V | Im |

B
| IVm | | Im | |

| IVm | | V | |

C
| Im | IVm | V | Im |

| Im | IVm | V | Im |

♩ = 112   *AEOLIAN MODE*   (suggested)

4

A
| Iadd9 | IIm7 | I/III | IVadd9 |

B
| V | IVadd9 | V | IVadd9 |

| V | IVadd9 | V | IV/V |

C
| Iadd9 | IIm7 | I/III | IVadd9 |

| Iadd9 | IIm7 | V | Iadd9 |

IMPROVISATIONAL CHORD PROGRESSIONS 5

choose your own keys

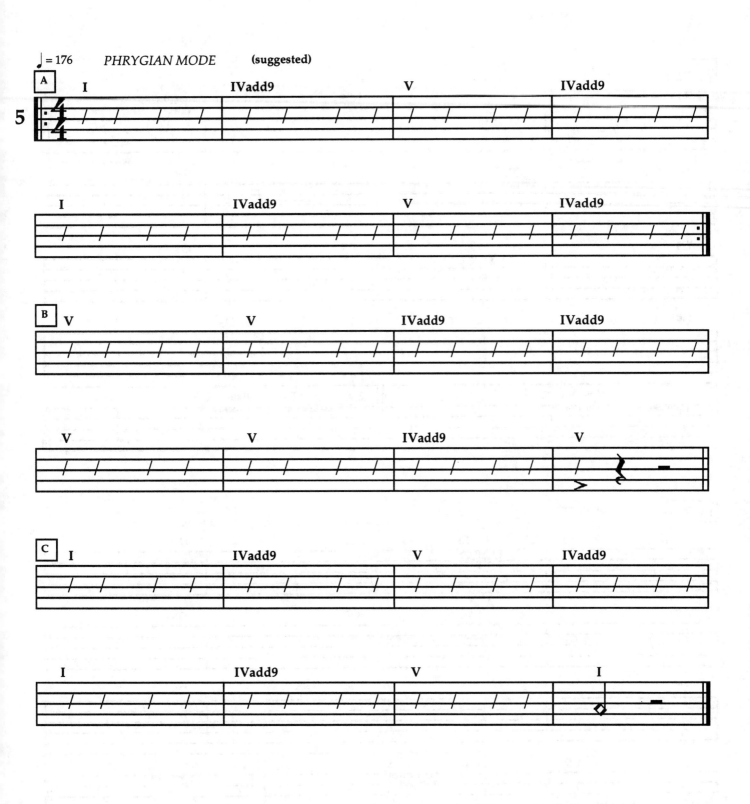

12 BAR BLUES TIMES TWO

choose your own keys and use the blues scale or minor pentatonic scale to improvise

♩ = 112 or ♩ = 60 (for triplet feel)

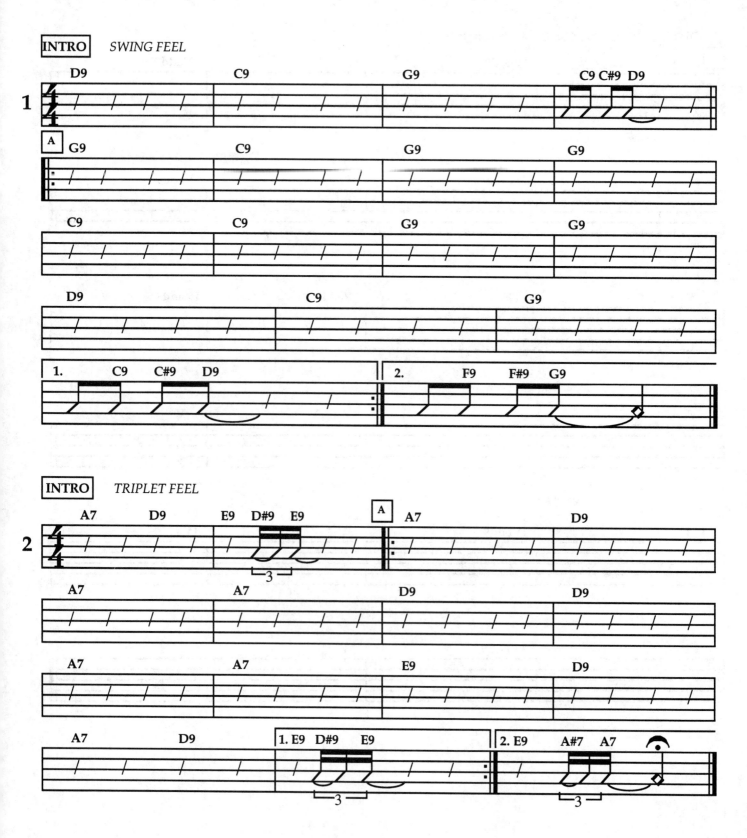

12 BAR BLUES TIMES TWO—CHORDS

D9
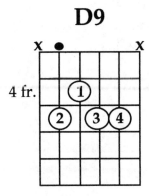

C9
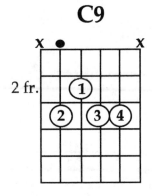

G9
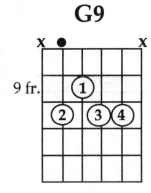

C#9
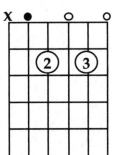

F9
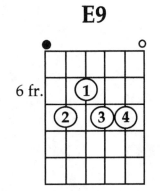

F#9
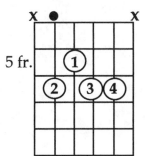

A7
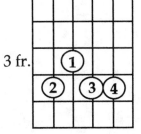

E9
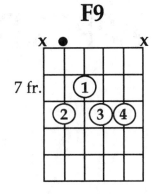

D#9
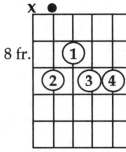

A#7
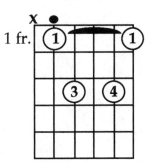

x = do not play   o = play open   ● = root (bass) note   4 fr. = fret number   ━━━ = barre chord

APPENDICES

THE KEYS

The Cycle of 5ths: There is an interval of a fifth (3 1/2 steps) between each of the following keys.

key of **C** to key of **G** example: **C**   D   E   F   **G**

count up the scale: **1**   2   3   4   **5**

Using the *cycle of 5ths* (beginning with the key of C) will help you to remember the key names and number of sharps or flats in each.

KEY	NUMBER OF SHARPS (#) or FLATS (♭)	
C	**0** sharps or flats	
G	**1** sharp	(F#)
D	**2** sharps	(F#, C#)
A	**3** sharps	(F#, C#, G#)
E	**4** sharps	(F#, C#, G#, D#)
B (C♭—7 flats)	**5** sharps	(F#, C#, G#, D#, A#)
F# (G♭—6 flats)	**6** sharps	(F#, C#, G#, D#, A#, E#)
C# (D♭—5 flats)	**7** sharps	(F#, C#, G#, D#, A#, E#, B#)
A♭	**4** flats	(B♭, E♭, A♭, D♭)
E♭	**3** flats	(B♭, E♭, A♭)
B♭	**2** flats	(B♭, E♭)
F	**1** flat	(B♭)

GUITAR FINGER BOARD NOTES

String Number:	6	5	4	3	2	1
Open String Name:	E	A	D	G	B	E
fret number 1	F	A#	D#	G#	C	F
fret number 2	F#	B	E	A	C#	F#
fret number 3	G	C	F	A#	D	G
fret number 4	G#	C#	F#	B	D#	G#
fret number 5	A	D	G	C	E	A
fret number 6	A#	D#	G#	C#	F	A#
fret number 7	B	E	A	D	F#	B
fret number 8	C	F	A#	D#	G	C
fret number 9	C#	F#	B	E	G#	C#
fret number 10	D	G	C	F	A	D
fret number 11	D#	G#	C#	F#	A#	D#
fret number 12	E	A	D	G	B	E

GUITAR OPEN TUNINGS

STRING NUMBER:

6	5	4	3	2	1
(lowest)					(highest)

STANDARD TUNING:

E	A	D	G	B	E

LOW SIXTH STRING:

D	A	D	G	B	E

OPEN "G" TUNING:

D	G	D	G	B	D

OPEN "D" TUNING:

D	A	D	F#	A	D

NOTE: Always open tune DOWN to avoid excess tension on guitar neck and bridge.

TEN TOP TIPS FOR TIGHT TEAMS

1. **Know your own voice or instrument.** (breathing, phrasing, tone, diction, chord voicings and shapes, scales, modes, licks & tricks)

2. **Warm up first (spiritually & musically).** Don't worship "cold."

3. **Use an electronic tuner for all tunable instruments.**

4. **Use high quality gear.** Use a regular maintenance schedule: change batteries & strings, set intonation, tune piano, new sticks & picks, etc.

5. **Pay attention to vocal and instrument arrangements:**

   <u>vocal harmonies</u>: Make a "lead vocal sandwich."
   low = alto (fifth above the melody, dropped an octave)
   mid = melody (lead vocal—male or female)
   high = tenor (third above the melody)

   <u>two guitars</u>: One plays rhythmic strums or finger picking while the other plays leads, licks, and fills.

   <u>two keyboards</u>: One plays "piano style" arpeggios, fills, and chords (not too heavy or low with left hand), while the other plays "pads" (strings, organ, legato parts).

   <u>drums/percussion</u>: Drums cover the basic rhythm and some fills. Percussion covers alternate rhythms, fills, and syncopation.

   <u>bass guitar/kick drum</u>: They generally play the <u>same</u> rhythm.

6. **Check the key signature (number of sharps & flats).** Watch out for chromatics!

7. **Modulate (change key) together.**

8. **Follow the leader.** Watch for hand signals and other direction.

9. **Be dynamic.** Rise and fall with the music/worship, let it breathe.

10. **Less is more.** Leave holes for improvisational prophetic expression by inspiration. Let the other guy have a chance! **No "lick" hogs!**

SONGS & MUSICAL TERMS

CHORD
DIAGRAMS

IN CLOSING

Mission Statement

The mission of Worship Works! is to honor and glorify God with contemporary praise and worship by reaching out to the unsaved and leading the saved into the presence of the Almighty.

Foundational Scripture

"For we are His workmanship, created in Christ Jesus for good works, which God prepared beforehand that we should walk in them."

Ephesians 2:10

Questions?

E-mail: *essentialworship@aol.com*

Website: *www.worshipworksmusic.com*

"because worship is essential"